Angels, Thieves, and Winemakers

Also by Joseph Mills

Angels, Thieves, and Winemakers

SECOND EDITION

Joseph Mills

Press 53
Winston-Salem

Press 53, LLC
PO Box 30314
Winston-Salem, NC 27130

Second Edition

Cover design by Kevin Morgan Watson

Cover art, "Dark Field Wine Glass (Explore #35 – December 30,
2012)," Copyright © 2012 by Calvin James,
used by permission of the artist.
www.CalvinJamesPhotography.com

Printed on acid-free paper
ISBN 978-1-941209-22-6

For Danielle

Acknowledgments

The author wishes to thank the following publications where many of these poems (or earlier versions) have appeared: *American Wine Society Journal*, *ChangeSeven*, *Enopoetica*, *Foliate Oak*, *The Inquisitive Eater*, *Iodine Poetry Journal*, *Latitude*, *Main Street Rag*, *Muscadine Lines*, *New Works Review*, *North Carolina Literary Review*, *Rattle*, *Santa Clara Review*, *Small Winery Magazine*, *The Writer's Almanac* with Garrison Keillor, and *Your Daily Poem*.

Contents

We hear of the conversion of water into wine at the marriage in Cana as of a miracle. But this conversion is, through the goodness of God, made every day before our eyes. Behold the rain which descends from heaven upon our vineyards, and which incorporates itself with the grapes, to be changed into wine; a constant proof that God loves us, and loves to see us happy.

—Benjamin Franklin

Wine goes in/ truth comes out.

—Harmonica Frank

Introductions Made Easy

If only people wore labels,
their foreheads clearly displaying
their appellation, their varietal,
their alcohol content,
think of the time it would save.
We could cut out the small talk,
the "Where are you from?"
and "What do you do?"
Appropriate pairings
would be more obvious.
We might know if they met
government standards,
and we would have a better idea
who might improve with age
and who we should enjoy
right now.

Aging

To speak of a wine's future
is to speak of our own desires,
how we hope as we age
that we'll become more
harmonious, less acidic,
that our tannins will mellow.
We recognize right now
we have a burst of flavor,
an energy, a liveliness,
but also a harshness
which later may soften
until we're more balanced,
more approachable,
easier to appreciate.
Hold onto us;
we believe
we'll get better.

The Good Nights

On the good nights,
when the bottle's empty,
we always want
just a little more,
half a glass,
a few sips,
a taste.
We know this desire
can be dangerous
to pursue,
that it can make
mornings difficult,
so usually we
brush our teeth
let the dog in,
lock the doors,
but sometimes,
even as we say,
*We really should
get ready for bed,*
instead of loading
the dishwasher
we will search
for the corkscrew,
all the while
shaking our heads
in wonder
at this willingness
to ignore the clocks
and the fact we have
to work tomorrow,
this irresponsibility,
this evidence,
even after all these years,
of the unquenchable desire
for each other's company.

Twenty Years Later I Make a Realization about Her Shampoo

What do you smell,
the winemaker asks,
and I hesitate to answer
because it's an old girlfriend
and weekends in her studio apartment,
milk carton bookshelves,
cracked walls, and ceilings
whose stains we pretended formed maps
of countries like Mythica and Fornucopia.
He waits politely,
but you can't say
you smell a lover,
broken plaster,
old jokes,
a life you used to have.

Finally, he suggests,
Grapefruit?
and I realize, yes,
that's it,
the nape of her neck,
her ears,
her hair.
Grapefruit.

Why You Should Have Your Date Open the Bottle

You can tell a lot about people
by what they drink
when they're alone,
how they react to spills
or others sipping from their glass,
and, especially, by what they do
when faced with a broken cork.
Some recognize this happens,
and some rail against their fate.
Some extract the shattered pieces
with the delicacy of surgeons,
others ask for advice,
and a few punch the cork
into the bottle, heedless
of the wine spurting
like blood from a broken nose.

So perhaps on a first date
what would be best
isn't a sunset walk along a beach,
but a meal where candles
light the tablecloth on fire,
a mixed up food order
triggering an allergic reaction,
a slip that sprains an ankle,
something requiring an ambulance;
you should hope
for a cork to shear,
so you can see how
you both might deal
with the breakage
that will be an inevitable part
of your lives together.

A Corkscrew Is an Instrument of Optimism

The labels warn about the dangers of drinking
and driving, drinking and being pregnant,
drinking and operating heavy machinery,
but they're silent about the dangers of drinking
and emailing or texting or Facebooking.
They don't caution you about how drinking
may result in spills that lead to sprained ankles,
or twisted knees or wrenched backs.
There's not a word about how drinking
can result in wardrobe malfunctions,
crippling humiliations, and broken friendships.

Why isn't the surgeon general concerned
with these? Why aren't we being warned
how drinking may cause us to try to kiss
strangers and other people's partners?
Why isn't there a statement, "Caution:
Truth may not be as close as it appears"?
Why don't the labels clearly explain drinking
can lead to speaking too much and too openly,
that effects include the temptation to undress
yourself and others, that it may stimulate
a desire to uncover long-hidden desires;
in short, that drinking may reveal
what probably should remain hidden?

The problem is no label is big enough
to include all the necessary admonitions,
so maybe there should be some type
of Drinker's Ed or a license requirement.
And, there could be alcohol insurance
covering accidents from falls to pregnancies.
Or, perhaps the best solution would be
to simply wrap each bottle in a waiver,
that must be signed before the cork is pulled,
a disclaimer certifying we understand
the diverse dangers involved in drinking and
the almost-infinite risk in being who we are.

Some Questions about the Drinking Habits of Angels

Angel's Share:The wine in oak barrels that disappears due to evaporation.

i.

How do angels get their shares?
Do they sip them straight from the casks,
pressing celestial lips against the bungs,
or do they siphon into the equivalent
of heavenly hip flasks and mason jars?
Do they line up so it's first come, first serve,
or are lesser angels relegated to table wines
while the seraphim hover over the reserves?

And what do they do with their shares?
Do they drink them in a winery crawl
until their wings are stained purple,
and they start speaking indiscreetly
about office politics and their belief
they should be ascending more quickly?
Or do they save them for later,
to taste and make notes like *Earthy,*
vegetal. Not as good as the 1503
but much better than the 1884,
halos bobbing in spirited harmony.

ii.

Are angels tempted to send rain
or sunshine, to beat their wings
to cool the nights, to whisper
It's time into a winemaker's dreams?
Do they nod or grimace at decisions,
like fans following favorite teams,
or are they as indifferent as nurses
drawing blood? Perhaps taking wine
is simply a job like guarding, glorifying,
or avenging. It may not be as gratifying
as delivering pregnancy announcements,
but it keeps them busy and out of trouble.

iii.

What if they're taking
more than wine?
Think of all the hours
and days and years
that seem to disappear.
Maybe the answer to
"Where does the time go?"
isn't that we waste or lose it,
but that it is being stolen,
sipped away by angels.

iv.

What if the angels aren't drinking
their shares, but are saving them,
so that later, when we check-in,
or perhaps at judgment day,
we'll find samples of all the wines
and all the days, all the lost friendships,
all we thought had evaporated away,
lined up, not as an appreciation
or a rebuke, but simply a testament,
to what we tried to make with our lives.

Bibiana, the Patron Saint of Hangovers

She must find it irritating how we only ask for help
afterwards instead of when we're opening another bottle
or closing another bar; yet, no one prays to Christopher
at the end of the trip. It's too late then. And it must be
annoying that so few of us pray to her by name;
instead, we try to go right to the top—*Oh Jesus, Oh God,*—
or we moan supplications to no recipient at all.

Since her responsibilities include epileptics, the insane,
torture victims, and the diocese of Los Angles,
she probably gets impatient with those whose sufferings
are self-inflicted. And she must find it frustrating when
the successes of her coworkers, like Vincent and Urban,
increase her work load. So, an apology and a prayer
for December 31, March 16, the hour before Happy Hour…

*Oh, Saint Bibiana, remember what it felt like to be human
and watch over us as we make our way among the bottles.
Keep us safe from the dangers of mixed drinks, sulfites,
and having one more for the road. In the morning,
or whenever we may awake, let our heads be small
and our regrets smaller. Please, Saint Bibiana, protect us,
pray for us, and forgive us for making you work so hard.
Amen.
Thanks.
And cheers.*

The Gospel According to Bob

If only one apostle would have had
a more Parker-like palate,
and a little professional distance,
then, at times like the wedding,
when Jesus turned water into wine,
while everyone marveled,
he might have stayed calm
and offered a rational report
for *The Galileen Gourmand*
such as "Golden. Fig tones.
But lacking body. An 87."

DaVinci's *Last Supper* suggests
they tried, showing them arguing
about flavor profiles and ratings,
but it was just for appearances
since they almost all gave raves,
influenced by such close access
to the maker and the tagline,
"This is my blood."

But maybe one day we'll find
sealed in some desert cave
scrolled notes in a clay pitcher,
and we will finally have
a gospel with no ambiguities,
just a few evocative adjectives
and a single decisive number.

Proust in the Tasting Room

The winemaker passes around vials
and asks us to identify the scents.
I recognize some: leather and lilac,
pepper and ... *is that cat pee?*
Others seem familiar, but elusive,
then there's lemon and suddenly
my mother's thin hands drying dishes
at the sink overlooking the alley,
and my father's coat steeped in tobacco
and the mildew of Mary's basement
where she taught me that kissing
was whistling without blowing.

Years ago I lived in a building that smelled
of fried onions and latex paint, and one Sunday
the old woman next door, who trailed clouds
of musky rose perfume, had a heart attack.
As the EMS guys wheeled her to the elevator,
I heard them complain about missing the game.
Do winemakers have to harden themselves
like ambulance drivers, surgeons, or strippers?
Before starting work, do they hang their memories
in some mental locker? They must do something
so the smell of lemon evokes only lemon.
Otherwise how are they not overwhelmed
by their lives pouring out under their noses.

The Fine Art of Blending

The stranger next to us
contemplates his glass, swirls,
sniffs, then swirls and sniffs again.
Finally he sips and says something
about the feel or fruit, the finish or flux,
how hints of leather and lace
almost mask the floral and fauna qualities
which are, of course, the varietal's signature.
The judgment snaps into place
with the snugness of a child-proof cap
sealing an aspirin bottle.

He contemplates us,
so we swirl and sniff,
then swirl and sip,
trying to make it seem
our mouths are full
of sensitive dials and gauges
when, in fact, we have only two:
a green LIKE IT! light
and a red DUMP IT! one.

Hmmm, I finally say, *Hmmm*.
and you tilt your head,
give a reticent smile, and add,
*You would have to be careful
how you pair it.*

Yes, the man nods, *Yes*,
satisfied with this sample
of our discernment,
content to be in our company.

Tasting Names

Sample the names.

Tuscany
Tumbarumba

Hold them in your mouth.
Swish them through your teeth.

Carneros
Coonawara

Taste the soft vowels,
the crisp consonants,
the spice of accents and umlauts.
Feel your tongue become thick.

Rheingau
Penedés

Savor the places you've been
or want to go.

Mendocino
> *Montrachet*
> > *Mendoza*

Imagine the vineyards,
the hills, the waters,
the suns and rains and fogs.

Medoc

Say the names out loud
in the store aisles
in the tasting rooms
in the middle of the night.

Alsace

Whisper them
into the dark

Emillion . . . Languedoc . . . Alentejo

as if they're lovers
or prayers for lovers.

The Teetotaler States Her Objections

It's not just the ogling and smelling,
the fingering and cupping of curves,
the anticipation of the first time
in the mouth, the giddy infatuations,
the constant fix-ups by friends
wantonly passing their pleasures around,
and it's not the expense, the ridiculous prices,
the pretentiousness or pompousness,

it's that there's no expectation
of a long-term commitment.
A bottle may barely last a night.
Worse are demi-bottles, flings by design,
a moment together with no future,
no fear of consequences.
It's all sensuality with no monogamy.
And the dump bucket?
What kind of callousness is that?
If you don't like one,
toss it and try another.

And even if you do find one
you love and respect and admire,
one that you want to be with,
one that makes a pleasing pairing,
even then you're not satisfied,
even then you keep looking
and shamelessly sampling others
... even then ... even then ...

At Happy Hour, She Offers a Half Dozen Hypotheses Why a
Second Glass Can Taste Better

1) The eye sees the refill
and tells the body,
Hey, we're staying
for a while.
Relax.

2) The wine itself relaxes;
having slipped out of its cork corset,
it begins to breathe easier
and make itself more sociable.
After all, if you were bottled up
for months, even years,
you'd be a little shy
or irritable at first.

3) You've made the decision
to spend more time
with those at the table,
and when you stop thinking
of excuses to leave,
you enjoy things more.

4) You are wiser
than a glass ago.
There is no mystery now
about what the bottle holds.
You no longer have expectations
or illusions
but you still have
desire.

5) You still have desire.

6) Desire.

Nouveau

Moving from the couch towards the bed,
they knock over a glass and splash wine
onto the rug, their discarded clothes, the wall.
Should this happen in years to come,
when their passion has aged and deepened,
they might disentangle, turn on the lights,
and search for towels and salt to clean up,
but now, now they barely notice the spill,
drunk on the exhilarating newness,
the sharp pleasure of this fresh pressing.

Every Beach Is an Unassembled Armonica

She wets a finger and caresses
the rim of a thrift store glass
until it starts to ring like crystal,
and he imagines what might happen
if she were to take his heart
into those hands and circle
its edges with her fingertips,
how it might vibrate, hum,
and finally burst into song.

As He Pours Wine He Tells Us

. . . how Leif Ericson landed in North America
around 1000 AD and called it "Vinland";
how Gutenberg first used an old wine press;
how King Dagobert was so infatuated
with a woman he built pipelines to bring her
the whites and reds of her native town;
how Winston Churchill exhorted,
"Gentlemen, remember, it's not just France
we are fighting for, it's Champagne!";
how a Greek man saved his house
from fire by drenching it with wine,
how Jesus and Dionysus, Zeus and Osiris,
Buddha and Shiva, held similar glasses . . .

This, he says, this is what you're drinking.

Standing in a Vineyard with a Grower Who Explains Some Reservations He Wishes Were More Widely Shared

A grape should be difficult to crush.
Not physically, any more than it's hard
to break an egg or smash a pumpkin,
but you should always be reticent to rupture
a container that gives coherence to chaos.

Consider the shape: a sphere, an orb, a globe,
the same as the planets and the stars.
Since this is the form the universe wants
material to take, we should be careful
destroying it thinking we can do better.

Thieves

When winemakers use the thief,
a long pipette, to withdraw liquid
from a cask or carboy,
it looks as if they're performing
exploratory surgery to determine
the state of what's inside,
but consider the name of the tool.

Consider how you would stop
and look through the classroom window
at your child's daycare and school.

Consider the expressions of painters
after they've sold canvases
they've worked on for months
or of chefs in kitchens after midnight.

What we make is not ours;
someday our rooms will be empty,
love makes thieves of us all.

In a Tasting Room Every Year Is a Good Year

The staff trumpets virtues and delights
until they are as credible as singles ads
and as tedious. How refreshing it would be
to hear an almost praisesong: "It's as good
as we could do this year with what we had,"
or "Perfect to give a colleague who knows
little of wine, but will like the blue bottle."
Roadside markers could serve as a model,
the way they offer information such as,
"In 1774 George Washington camped
three miles west" or "A mile east of here
there once was something of significance."
Who wouldn't appreciate the honesty
of a label that said, *This vintage is close
to something noteworthy. It's very close.*

A Winemaker Defends His Craft as He Pours Yet More Samples

Some of the Baptist neighbors
don't like that he's started a winery,
but what they don't understand
is that fermentation occurs in nature,
which means drinking occurs in nature
so there's nothing wrong
or sinful about it,
and for proof he lists
some of the drunk animals he's known,
like a friend's dog in college
who would have a couple beers each night
then lie by the door and howl,
although maybe this isn't the best example
but there are plenty of other ones
because grapes will turn to alcohol
all by themselves
which means it must be
the way God wants it
and animals naturally find them
and eat them and feel the effects—
that's why there are so many
stories about raccoons
passing out in garbage cans,
squirrels falling off tree limbs,
deer and birds and bees
staggering around.
You can name any animal
and he's seen or heard or read
something that proves
they like to drink—
and that includes horses
cows, pigs, goats, chickens—
although he recognizes
that, strictly speaking,
these might not be considered natural,
if by natural people mean wild,

which is not what he means.
He means all animals,
living creatures,
God's creatures.
Gods and animals
get drunk
because there's wine
in the wilderness
because fruit ferments naturally,
and people just help it along,
like planting corn
or wheat or soybeans.
No one says
that it's unnatural,
to grow corn,
do they? Do they?

Of course not.
Winemaking is just
helping nature along,
and if you say it's wrong,
you're saying
God is wrong
because Jesus didn't turn
water into orange juice
or milk or Gatorade,
he turned it into wine
and the only question
is whether it was red
or white and, frankly,
although he probably shouldn't say this
because it might upset some people,
he would bet that God the Father
is more of a red wine drinker,
particularly in the old testament,
but Jesus strikes him
as more partial to white.

Either way, there's no question
that wine is
the most natural thing
in the world
because, who makes it?
God.
And who drinks it?
Animals.

A Winemaker Talks about America

With this machine, you can filter a wine
so much you can take the color right out,
and that's what some people want.
Something that looks clear and clean,
no sediment or tartrates or taste.
It goes with the mania for single varietals
and the prejudice against blends.
Those age-old delusions and fantasies
of purity. Sure, you need to be careful
pruning and pressing. But this machine?
It's the most dangerous one here.

American Beaujolais

When it arrived,
I was in a Vegas coffee shop
trying not to listen
to the next table,
the loud woman in sunglasses,
the loud man with thick fingers,

Why can't I
for once?
Why not?

He orders the waitress
to take back her food,
although she insists,

It's okay. Stop it.
It's fine. Damnit.

But even they quiet
when the pompadoured waiter
begins a solemn weave
around the tables,
the new currency
displayed
between his hands.

It's the hundred, see?
Have you seen it?
See?

Explaining to the family from Jersey
the markings, the differences,
as they pass it around,
like a baby photo,
oohing and ahing,

Then in 17 weeks,
the fifties.
Then in 17 weeks,
the twenties.
Then in 17 weeks . . .

A bus boy asks
if he can show the guys
in the kitchen.

Okay, but be careful
and bring it back.
Bring it back soon.

Westernly

In Albuquerque,
I would do laundry
across from a liquor store
with a drive-up window,
and as I sorted and folded uniforms,
I would watch trucks,
low-riders, and station wagons
circle the building,
like case studies
in laziness and irresponsibility.

Then one evening I saw a rider
walk his horse around the store.
He took the six pack
pushed through the window,
opened a can,
hooked the rest
on the saddle horn,
and rode into the darkness,

and I thought, *Ohhhhh,*
and, like a child, I thought,
I want a horse,
and like the poet
in the Maverick Bar,
I thought, *America
I could almost love you,*
and I thought, *My life
has gone wrong,*
and I thought,
America my life ohhh.

Wile E Coyote Circles the Winery Aisles, His Optimism a Pure Distillation of the American Dream

He scrutinizes the labels
as if they're mysteries to be solved,
and he can determine what happened:
who did what, where, and when.
But really the question he's trying to answer,
by decoding the vintages and varietals,
the tasting notes and talking points, is

Which one?
           Which one?
                      Which one?

which one will help him catch
that elusive road runner of desire?
He's confident it can be done
if he just makes the right choice
and has enough money to buy it.
This is the pursuit of happiness,
a Moebius strip of yearning,
a Merrie Melodie of canine hunger.

The Store Owner Explains What's Being Sold in a Wine Aisle

Here, the overwhelming geography
of countries and territories,
regions and sub-regions,
is clearly, neatly, organized.

Here, the messy histories
of families and governments,
migrations and movements,
are given clean, brief, stories.

Here, a year's weather
and work is distilled
to a few simple numbers.

Here is a world
designed to be navigated
bottle by bottle,
one eager to be consumed
by people like us.

Cave Men

A full wine rack is
Saturday mornings,
the first day of vacation,
a just-waxed car.
It is a promise of future good dinners,
of future celebrations,
of a future.

A full wine rack murmurs:
Don't worry.
There's plenty.
You're safe.

The Server, Still Unsure about the Pregnancy, Considers the Utility of the Wine Menu's Basic Principle

Regardless of the varietal or vintage,
the winery or winemaker,
selections become more expensive
as you go down the list.

If only our lives were like this.
If only we had some idea
how much each choice,
each pleasure, will cost
when the bill comes due,
if only we knew how far
we could afford to descend.

His Daughter, Who Has Just Been Dumped, Recognizes
That He Is, in His Way, Trying to Help

A wine can be special one year and mediocre the next.
A freeze or too much rain may damage the crop.
The winemaker might crush too early or too late.
There's so much that can go wrong with the grapes,
the tanks, the barrels, the bottling, it's amazing
anything pleasurable to drink ever gets made.

So, John '12 might be buoyant and bright,
while John '13 might be shit. Maybe the weather
of his life—disease or deaths—caused disruptions.
Some years, all goes right, and we're good company;
some years we end up thin, harsh, disappointing.
What we need most isn't a palate, but a patience
and a recognition that time brings new releases
even of those we thought we knew well.

A Glass is a Temporary Arrangement of Shards

It's clear he doesn't recognize the silverware
and glassware arrayed around his plate,
so a coiffed woman seated nearby
tries to reassure him by insisting manners
are simply a code designed to keep people
from attacking and killing each other.
You can feel it, she says, at every toast.
As you raise your drink into the air,
there's the delicious temptation to thrust
into a shattering. So, each clink of crystal
is a demonstration of trust, a sign
that we're mastering our violent desires,
a pledge we will refrain, at least for now,
from jamming our forks and fingers
into the flesh so temptingly within reach.

On the Way to Montserrat, Following Parsifal, We Stopped to Picnic

No one remembered to pack glasses,
so we had to drink from the bottle,
and two of us were content
to swap swigs as we ate sandwiches,
but the third was hesitant,
not for sanitary reasons
or a concern with fairness,
but because of how it looked
to people going by.
At her turn, she would crouch,
hunch towards the car
and upend the bottle
as quick as a thief
pocketing a tip from a table.

Years later, I'm still sharing wine,
with the woman who laughed
and stood upright. We travel now
with our children, whom we hope
are polite without staying silent
about suffering. Our friend long ago
disappeared into time's woods.
Perhaps she found companions
with impeccable manners;
perhaps she's still searching
for a place wine is served in chalices
precisely the way she imagines
the attention of others requires.

The Minister Talks to the Couple Before the Ceremony

Despite what friends and experts may say,
no one really knows what the years will do.
Some turn to vinegar. Some crack or become
corked, and some simply don't age well.
All you can do is try to avoid extremes,
create a safe environment, and check in regularly.
If you're lucky, your patience and protection
will allow for the development of a richness
and complexity, so that decades from now,
you'll be able to savor something special.
The value then will be obvious to everyone,
but only you will truly understand what it cost.

The Sweet Ones

After work, they meet at the grocery,
grab two carts, drop a child in each,
and begin speed-walking the aisles,
pausing only in the liquor section
where a distributor has set up a table
offering samples of dessert wine.
There, while they try to keep the kids
from boarding one another's carts,
they pretend to listen to the spiel
about thickness, viscosity, sweetness,
how *The Aussies call them "stickies,"*
how a small glass should be sipped
as the luxurious conclusion to a meal.
They knock back everything on offer
as if auditioning for a saloon scene,
then race on to the frozen foods.

That night, once they've scrubbed
the accumulation of dirt and sugar
from the kid's faces, put them to bed,
then put them back to bed,
once they've washed the dishes,
swept the floors, and prepared
for the next day's obligations,
they turn off the lights and sit
on the porch swing, sharing
a piece of chocolate and savoring
the luxurious quiet. Finally
one of them asks, "Fancy a sticky?"
momentarily puzzling the other
since they didn't buy any wine,
then, clasping hands, they rise
and wend their way together
through the house's soft darkness.

The Boat in the Bottle

When you uncork an Australian wine,
you might get a faint whiff
of sea salt and sweat,
of the hunger and fear of those
in the long boats from the First Fleet.
And sometimes when you hold a glass
to the light, you can see them,
the thieves and perjurers,
the fraudsters and deserters,
each carrying against his chest
a twig in a small cloth sack,
a vinifera rootstock thinner
than the finger bone of a saint.

Lessons

My four-year-old daughter holds up her sippy cup.
Chin Chin, Daddy, she says, and everyone laughs,
except me because I'm thinking how this will hurt
if she becomes an alcoholic or pregnant at sixteen.
I'm imagining the state trooper coming to the door.
But then I do the same as I teach her how to cartwheel,
picturing the future neck-breaking fall off the beam,
or how to walk the dog that can yank her into traffic,
or how to demonstrate anything in the kitchen
with its knives, flames, edges, grinders and glass.

My daughter has revealed the world is a deathtrap,
and I want to lock her in an empty room and feed her
mashed bananas by hand instead of wondering
what pleasurable moment will haunt me later
and which of these lessons I will end up regretting.
But I am learning to swallow the constant fear,
so I smile, say, *Chin Chin, Baby Girl,* and click my glass
against her plastic cup while everyone goes *Awwww.*

Requirements for Earning a Few Common, but Lesser-Known, Merit Badges

Blending: When your parents host a party, help clear away the dishes. Pretend you don't hear the adults commenting on your nice manners. Collect the cups that still have wine. Screen them for cigarette butts, matches, toothpicks, peanut shells, then dump them into a pitcher, preferably one that's opaque. Later, pour this into your regulation silver canteen with its detachable canvas cover and genuine Boy Scouts of America logo, the one that was a hand-me-down from your cousin. Stash this in the tent you and Johnny have set up behind the garage.

Drinking: With Johnny, and maybe one or two other boys, but not Bobby, who would tell his Mom, pass the canteen around the way you've seen in movies. Accuse the others of hogging it even though when it's your turn you're just miming swallowing. Offer a few tasting notes like, *Damn, this is good.*

Conversing: Talk about the girls that you're supposed to like. Talk about who might be willing to buy cigarettes for you. Talk about how much you like girls and smoking. Talk about how much you like wine, and how you drink it all the time at home.

Acting: Once it gets late enough, stop pretending to drink and move on to the claim of being drunk. Put your hand up when the canteen comes near and say, *I've had way more than my share. Johnny can have the rest.* Put your head back. Close your eyes. Sway and smile slightly like you hear a great song in your head. Pretend to doze. After a while, say, *I'm so wasted. I need to go home.* Go inside, and make popcorn. Ask a parent if you can have some. Watch a *Star Wars* episode to try to decide what you'll be for Halloween.

The Vintner

We called him Grandpa Joe, the gnarled old man
who helped build all the houses on the block.
At eighty, when a saw sliced through his hand,
he wrapped it in a towel and finished work.
Each Christmas, we would bring him little gifts,
and he would have us come in for a drink.
He'd even hand out glasses to the kids.
My mom would frown. My dad would grin and wink.
His home-made wine was orange and burned the throat.
It seemed to taste of tacks or splintered wood.
I felt grown-up drinking something that hurt,
a sample of the world of work and wounds,
but it was years before I understood
the making and the sharing made it good.

Practicing to Be a Poet

My father would take me to hunt
for beer cans along back roads,
easing the truck along the shoulder
and stopping at each swatch of metal.
It didn't matter if a can was dented
or rusted, I was going for quantity,
trying to build a wall display
from floor to ceiling, like the one
in Steve Costello's basement
that he and his dad had bought
at flea markets and conventions,
an impressive display of cone tops,
flat tops, Iron City Steelers cans,
and entire Schmidt wildlife sets.

Whatever my father thought of this,
he would wait, seemingly patient,
smoking Kool after Kool, as I scrambled
around ditches, and he would admire
anything I scavenged from the weeds,
saying, "That looks like a good one,"
when I would clamber back to my seat
with another Stag or Hamm's or Blatz.
Steve said we were wasting our time,
that nothing collected this way had value,
and I knew he was probably right,
but as my father and I drove the berms,
with Paul Harvey on the radio
and me cantilevered out the window,
I would feel a sense of possibility
as if at any moment we might find something
rare and wondrous and worth keeping.

Riddle

When I left home, my father gave me
a split of champagne and the advice:
Always have a bottle so you're ready
to celebrate good luck when it comes.
I felt he was sharing
part of the code by which men live,
like, tip the bartender each round,
or don't talk at the urinal row,
and it made sense to be prepared
to make luck feel welcome
since it can go so many other places.
Over the years, each time
I could offer chilled champagne
to toast an announcement,
I felt proud at this tangible proof
that I knew how to live.

After my father died,
I find a bottle in his fridge,
so discolored by droppings
of butter and syrup,
years of leftovers stored above it,
that the label was illegible.
Was it some rare vintage
requiring an event more special
than a promotion, a retirement,
a son's wedding, a grandchild's arrival?
Had he stopped believing in luck,
or did he just no longer recognize
what it looked like?
Had the bottle been forgotten
as his eyesight deteriorated,
or had my mother's death
made it untouchable?

I donated his clothing,
distributed the photos
to family and friends,
gave away the furniture,
appliances, and kitchenware;
I kept only the bottle,
so now I have two champagnes
in my refrigerator;
one, new, clean and ready to be drunk,
nestled against another
that all the luck in one man's life
wasn't enough to open.

Dirt

Here's one of the dirty secrets of the industry. Those bubbles
whose hypnotic risings make champagne champagne? They form
on the surface of the glass at "nucleation sites" and these are not
defects or pits of the material, but rather "hollow and roughly
cylindrical exogenous cellulose fibres,"[1] or, in other words,
dirt. Dead cells. Microscopic dust, debris and detritus.
Perhaps we should be horrified at the fundamental
baseness of this luxury or maybe we
should be inspired by such
a transformation of grit
into glamour.
Either way
we can
learn
from the
industry's
PR
how people
can be
convinced
the rising
turbulence
within us,
the periodic
roiling
created by
impurities
we can
never
cleanse,
is something to consider
as desirable, even beautiful,
for the way it makes us sparkle.

[1] From "Effervescence in a glass of champagne: *A bubble story*" by Gérard Liger-
Belair and Philippe Jeandet, Laboratoire d'œnologie, faculté des sciences de
Reims, France

Traces

In the last years of her life,
her mother never wanted to get out
the wedding linens, keeping them
locked in a cabinet, but her daughter
uses them now, as often as she can,
for holidays, birthdays, and dinners,

and, when she spreads the tablecloth,
her fingers trace its faint dark bruises,
the stains from spills over the years,
and she tries to imagine those times
when her parents still drank red wine
together with an exuberance
and carelessness that would mark
their most precious possessions.

A Teacher Explains the Process

Each fall when the grapes arrive,
we sift and evaluate them,
trying to determine how best
to help them be what they can be.
Some are thin-skinned and delicate,
others gruff and independent.
Some need oak, others stainless steel.
No single process works for all,
so first we must identify what they are,
not what we wish they were.

We believe careful attention,
time, and the right environment,
can help develop character,
complexity, balance, and depth.
But, most of all, we have faith
that, even when we can't see it,
fundamental transformations,
ones bordering on miraculous,
are bubbling under the surface.

On Attending a High School Graduation

Looking at them
clustered together
in their black robes,
waiting for their names
to be called,
waiting to become
more distinct
versions of themselves,
I whisper *veraison*,
and if it makes you
uncomfortable to consider
these boys and girls
in terms of ripeness,
the fullness of fruit
waiting to be picked,
that's understandable,
because after all,
if we're honest,
there's a coldness
about walking a vineyard
and casting a calculating eye
at all those vines
waiting to be thinned,
all those grapes
waiting to be harvested,
all that fruit
waiting to be crushed,
transformed and packaged
for our future pleasures.

The Complexity of Wine

When we told the teenage house sitter,
"Help yourself to anything in the fridge,"
we didn't think to exempt the wine,
particularly the expensive Sauternes
a Parisian friend had hand-carried
through customs as a wedding present.

We were shocked when we realized
not only had she opened the bottle,
but then recorked and refoiled it,
something we discovered only because
she had put it on the shelf backwards.

We were unsure what to do.
Tell her we knew? Tell her mother
who had urged us to hire her?
We had been keeping it for years
because it was such a thoughtful gift,
one that required a special occasion,
and because Sauternes was a wine
that neither of us really liked to drink.

The Photograph Albums in the Living Room

The albums record the harvests,
the weddings and graduations,
the vacations when we didn't get sick
or end up in the emergency room.

There are no photos showing
the seasons of drought,
the struggle to sink roots
into gravel and sand
places nothing else would grow,
the times we were pruned
so close to the ground
we didn't think we'd survive.

In these pictures, everyone smiles.
In these albums are the good vintages
we have produced together;
this is the library of our lives.

When Will These Three

In the hotel bar, three women sip wine,
each tailored, coiffed, and manicured,
each clearly in an on-going relationship
with a dentist. They may be perfectly nice,
but suddenly I want to be drinking beer
from a red plastic cup, standing by a keg,
and listening to Mary and Julie and Laura
explain what a dumb ass I am for something
I've said or done recently, all of us lit
by more than the pallets burning nearby,
maybe by youth, maybe hope, or maybe,
although I didn't recognize it then, by love
that didn't involve scrabbling in a back seat.
It's an easy fortune to tell. There are people
in your past who one day you will long for
with such an intensity that it will make
bartenders ask if you're okay and women
become concerned enough about you
to move their glasses to a different table.

Harvest

After years of planning, planting, pruning,
tending first the idea and then the vines,
after the fingers blistered then calloused,
after evenings when you were too tired
to eat, after nights when you couldn't stop
calculating the costs in terms of tons,
bottles, acres, all that you've denied
your children, finally the grapes are ripe.
You walk the green rows, pulling off clusters
of fruit until juice covers your arms
attracting clouds of butterflies. Here is
your harvest: these clapping wings of color,
these sweet handfuls of temporary grace.

Opening Up

As the dinner progressed
people's comments
about each wine
became increasingly
ridiculous,
and when the woman beside me
praised the way a red
unfolded in the mouth,
I snorted so hard
I almost shot snot
onto my plate.
For the rest of the night
I made comments like

I love how this dessert
unfolds in my mouth.

      Could someone please
      unfold some more wine
      towards me?

   Excuse me
   while I go
   unfold myself
   in the bathroom.

Even drunk I knew
I was being rude
not only to the woman
but the host,
a doctor who had opened
several special bottles
whose prices were never mentioned
and somehow known by all,
but I didn't care
much for wine
or people
who faked appreciation
as payment for supper.

I can still see those bottles
decanted on the table,
and I wonder
what they were.
Had I won the equivalent
of a tasting lottery
only to toss the ticket away?
I had been young and tight,
as closed as a fist;
now I know more
about the complicated blends
people can be,
how some mask
their insecurities
behind polite words
and others with sarcasm,
how rudeness can taste
like cruelty
and how silence may not be
acquiescence, but generosity.

If we're lucky,
as the years unfold
we open up
until we reach a point
we can appreciate
one another's complexities
and even the tart irony
of finding yourself
at the table's next seat,
taking seriously,
so many of those things
you once mocked.

Sea Changes

In college I read the *Iliad* and *Odyssey*,
and, although I thought they could be shorter,
overall they were better than I expected.
I wrote papers, bestowing my approval,
received the grades that I deserved
(but still complained about), and,
after graduation, boxed up Homer
with Hemingway, Hesse, and those authors
whose names you drop to impress people,
but whose books you usually read
only when it's required.

The box survived decades of moves,
changes and turbulence,
and one day, alone
in yet another furnished room,
I began to reread its contents
as if deciding to drink wines
I had sampled long ago
and been cellaring ever since.

I discover the stories have become richer,
more complex and more immediate.
At twenty, I had noted my professor's explanations,
so when Dante found himself lost in a dark wood
in the middle of his life, I had scribbled
"means something more" in the margin;
now, I realize what that something more is,
just as on my return to Homer's epics,
rather than impatiently skipping
the repetitive descriptions,
I find myself moved
by the constant insistence
on the "wine dark sea."

Perhaps it's because I better understand
how all of us end up voyaging
across some similar vastness,
and no matter how well we navigate,
how heroically we act,
what stories we tell for protection,
at some point we find ourselves
shipwrecked, lost, far from home,
struggling to make it back
to the ones we love,
yet knowing even as we do so,
that they, like us,
are being irreparably transformed
by time's unavoidable tides.

Old Professors

One smoked cigars in the classroom.
Another had seminars meet at his house,
serving us beer and wine. A third
held office hours at the campus pub,
and if he became too drunk to remember
to take papers home, the bartenders,
all graduate students, would hold them
for when he returned. Such behavior
is inconceivable, even illegal, now.
And yet those old professors made us
want to learn by assuming we could
handle being around alcohol and smoke,
boorish behavior and intoxicating ideas.

On Continuing to Keep Wines That Have Peaked

When we know a wine is as good
as it will get, why are we reluctant
to open the last bottles, continually saying,
Not yet. Maybe later. Maybe next time?
Are we irrational optimists, telling ourselves
it'll be fine for a little while longer?
Are we in denial about the inevitable decay?
Or do some of us know exactly the choice
we're making, recognizing we all become
tired, flabby, unable to satisfy as fully as before,
and yet there still may be good moments
in the years to come. Having been together
for so long, perhaps we're more forgiving.
No, we're not as good as we once were,
but something pleasing enough remains
that makes it difficult to say goodbye.

When My Students Ask Why They Need Poetry

What should I say? Because maybe they don't.
Now. Or next year. Or ever. Poems won't get them
a job or raise. They might never feel a connection,
or need, or desire. And yet, one day, they might
find in the waiting room, at the banquet table,
along the road, or by the grave, a poem will say
what they cannot. So maybe they should consider
poetry a type of first aid kit or fire extinguisher,
insurance for emotional emergencies, something
you hope to never use, but should have around.

Or, if this seems too cynical, consider me
a kind of merchant offering poems like bottles
of fine wine, ones that can be stored away,
so after you've accomplished your goals
of money, fame, and love, and find you have time
for luxuries like literature, you'll discover,
a cellar of aged poems, waiting to be savored.
What should I say? Maybe this: Whatever
you think you will need and whatever you think
of poetry, take some. They don't cost much now,
or take up much space, and they may be worth
a great deal to you later if you should live
long enough to return to them. I hope you will.

Finish

Winemakers talk about "finish,"
the impression that lingers
in the mouth
after you've swallowed,
and it's a useful standard
for evaluating wine

and poems

        and people.

Before you turn away,
take a moment to consider
the aftertaste,
what still stays with you
and what you think
you'll remember later.

Joseph Mills doesn't remember specific wines as much as he does the people and places involved with drinking them: the Bordeaux studio apartment where he shared cheap bottles (and a few expensive ones) with the woman who would become his wife; Clos Pegase in Napa where his six-year-old niece watched him fixedly because, as she explained, "I heard drinking makes people go crazy"; and the back garden at Brittany where he has listened to his in-laws sing old Breton songs for hours.

Many of the poems in this collection originated as he and his wife, Danielle Tarmey, researched *A Guide to North Carolina's Wineries* (John F. Blair). He also has published five books of poetry with Press 53. Currently he teaches at the University of North Carolina School of the Arts where he holds an endowed chair, the Susan Burress Wall Distinguished Professorship in the Humanities.

CPSIA information can be obtained at www.ICGtesting.com
Printed in the USA
BVOW04s1705220315

392726BV00002B/15/P